Writers and Their Work: No. 21

THOMAS HARDY

by

R. A. SCOTT-JAMES

PUBLISHED FOR
THE BRITISH COUNCIL
and the NATIONAL BOOK LEAGUE
by LONGMANS, GREEN & CO.

Revised Price
2s. 6d. net

R. A. Scott-James, an authoritative critic of modern literature, is one of the best-known editors of our day. As a young man he joined the staff of the *Daily News*, and was literary editor of that paper from 1906 to 1912. Soon after he became editor of the *New Weekly*. He joined the Royal Artillery in the first world war, and served in France with distinction, winning the Military Cross. From 1919 to 1930 he was leader-writer on the *Daily Chronicle*. He later joined the *Spectator*, and in 1934 took over editorship of the *London Mercury* from Sir John Squire.

Mr. Scott-James has known nearly all the outstanding writers of his time, including Thomas Hardy (1840–1928) of whose work, particularly his novels and his Napoleonic poem, *The Dynasts*, he writes so discerningly in this essay. His critical works include *Personality in Literature*, *The Making of Literature*, and a masterly survey of *Fifty Years of English Literature*, published in 1951, which contains an assessment of Hardy's lyric poetry.

Bibliographical Series
of Supplements to 'British Book News'
on Writers and Their Work

★

GENERAL EDITOR
Bonamy Dobrée

THOMAS HARDY
from a painting by Augustus John *in the Fitzwilliam Museum, Cambridge*

THOMAS HARDY

(1840–1928)

by R. A. SCOTT-JAMES

PUBLISHED FOR
THE BRITISH COUNCIL
and the NATIONAL BOOK LEAGUE
BY LONGMANS, GREEN & CO., LONDON, NEW YORK, TORONTO

LONGMANS, GREEN & CO. LTD.
6 & 7 Clifford Street, London W.1
Boston House, Strand Street, Cape Town
531 Little Collins Street, Melbourne

LONGMANS, GREEN & CO. INC.
55 Fifth Avenue, New York 3

LONGMANS, GREEN & CO.
20 Cranfield Road, Toronto 16

ORIENT LONGMANS PRIVATE LTD.
Calcutta Bombay Madras
Delhi Vijayawada Dacca

First published 1951
Reprinted 1957

PR
4754
.S26

Printed in Great Britain at The Curwen Press, Plaistow, E.13

CONTENTS

THOMAS HARDY   *page* 7

A SELECT BIBLIOGRAPHY   37

INDEX OF SHORT STORIES   43

¶ THOMAS HARDY was born at Higher Bockhampton, Dorset, on 2 June 1840. He died on 11 January 1928 at Dorchester.

THOMAS HARDY

'SUDDENLY an unexpected series of sounds began to be heard in this place up against the sky. They had a clearness which was to be found nowhere in the wind, and a sequence which was to be found nowhere in nature. They were the notes of Farmer Oak's flute.'

Such were the notes which set the key in the early pages of *Far From the Madding Crowd*. They are the same notes which were heard as distinctly in *Under the Greenwood Tree* (1872), the first of Thomas Hardy's novels to win the attention of a large public, though the second in order of appearance. That book introduces us to a place, a scene, set in a region whose particularities were to be gradually unfolded in a series of novels, a region to become familiar in the mind's eye as the 'Wessex of Thomas Hardy', centred in the hamlets, villages, towns, woods, meadows, and heathland of Dorset, and overflowing into the adjoining counties. It is a countryside inhabited by country people living, for the most part, under the conditions which prevailed when Hardy was a boy. The character of the region and still more the habits of the people have suffered many changes since then; and these outer and inner changes, already perceptibly beginning a hundred years ago, are again and again linked with the tragedies of his heroes and heroines. But the memory of it is fixed for posterity as long as English fiction continues to be read. The 'Wessex' described by Hardy lives in the imagination more distinctly than any other region described by an English writer, perhaps any writer. Not thus do we know even the Scottish country described by Walter Scott. The Lake country associated with Wordsworth is to Hardy's Wessex as a poetic symbol is to a human reality—a reality charged with all that is intimate and poignant in human experience. Not only have we been made to see the wild expanse of Egdon Heath, the rich meadowland of Talbothays, where Tess milked her cows and

Angel Clare made love to her, the fir plantations and orchards of the Hintocks among which moved Giles Winterbourne and Marty South, the houses and streets and cornmarket of Casterbridge, frequented by all the farmers of the neighbourhood; but also we have become aware of these places as influences subtly entering into the lives of the men and women born and bred there, who inherit memories, habits, and instincts handed on through the centuries. Those born in the Hintocks, with 'an almost exhaustive biographical or historical acquaintance with every object, animate and inanimate, within the observer's horizon know all about those invisible ones of the days gone by, whose feet have traversed the fields which look so grey from the window; recall whose creaking plough has turned those sods from time to time; whose hands planted the trees that form a crest to the opposite hill; whose horses and hounds have torn through that underwood; what birds affect that particular brake; what bygone domestic dramas of love, jealousy, revenge, or disappointment have been enacted in the cottages, the mansions, the street or the green'.

This Wessex country, inhabited by simple people and the ghosts of their ancestors, and no less by living animals and trees and grasses,[1] is the background never wholly absent in Hardy's work, fiction or poetry.

What he says of Clym Yeobright, walking on Egdon Heath in *The Return of the Native*, might have been said of himself.

> If anyone knew the heath well, it was Clym. He was permeated with its scenes, with its substance, with its odours. He might be said to be its product. His eyes had first opened thereon; with its appearance all the first images of his memory were mingled; his estimate of life had been coloured by it; his toys had been the flint knives and arrow-heads which he found there, wondering why stones should 'grow' to such odd shapes; his flowers, the purple bells and yellow gorse; his animal kingdom, the snakes and croppers; his society, its human haunters.

[1] It is curious that song-birds occur rarely in the novels.

Hardy was born in 1840 in Higher Bockhampton, in the parish of Stinsford. His father was a stonemason and builder, who inherited from the grandfather a love of instrumental music and the care of the church choir; carol-singing at Christmas, as described in *Under the Greenwood Tree*, and festive occasions celebrated with jigs, hornpipes, reels, and other country dances, lived in the memory of the novelist; again and again in his novels his style acquires a wonderful liveliness where he tells the story of a dance. As a small child, Florence Hardy tells, he was 'of ecstatic temperament, extraordinarily sensitive to music'; he was so moved by some of the tunes that he had to dance on to conceal his weeping. In his childhood his life was never far from that of the folk; he lived continuously in Dorset till he was twenty-two, attending first the village school, then schools at Dorchester, and at the age of sixteen he began to study architecture under an architect much of whose work was concerned with church restoration. He read books omnivorously, studied Latin and French, and later, with the help of a friend, Greek; and wrote poetry. It was in Dorchester that he came to know William Barnes, who as pedagogue gave him advice on grammar, and as poet stimulated his poetic interest in Dorset.

In literature, poetry was Hardy's first love, as it was his last. When he went to London at the age of twenty-two to pursue his profession of architecture, he worked conscientiously at it but continued to write poetry, though he had no success in getting it published. He was by no means unpractical. His supreme interest, he felt, lay in the composition of poetry, and throughout his earlier and middle creative period he constantly wrote verse to please himself; but he did not turn his back on the necessity of earning a living. He continued his regular work as an architect until he had made sure that he could succeed in literature; and in the field of literature, since the editors and publishers did not want his poems, but did, in time, come to demand his novels, he gave his energies to fiction and found there his means of self-expression. He was to prove that a poet could write fiction in prose and would do it the better for being a poet. But often the task was irksome. Many of his novels had to be written to time to suit the journals in which they were published serially; when he was at the height of his powers (aged forty-six) he complained that his novel-writing was 'mere journeywork', and in later years he was impatient with those who did not think his verse superior to his fiction. But one need not overstress this self-criticism. Earlier, he was dissatisfied with cramping conditions; later, enjoying freedom, he remembered years when he had written under duress. Again and again he spoke seriously enough of his art, meaning the art of fiction, as when he wrote in his Memoranda: 'My art is to intensify the expression of things, as is done by Crivelli, Bellini, etc., so that the heart and inner meaning is made vividly visible' (1886).

None the less, one must remember that for more than twenty years, during most of his novel-writing period, Hardy was, in a certain sense, writing for a living; that is to say, he was not in a position to rest on his oars and stop writing. This means that though we shall see him developing his essential powers and writing from inner necessity, we shall also find him producing work in which he is below himself, in books parts at least of which are irrelevant to his genius. His first venture in fiction, *The Poor Man and the Lady*, was never published, though a much shortened version of it was printed later in a magazine. It was read and criticized by two publishers' readers, none other than John Morley and George Meredith, the latter advising him, probably rightly, against publication, but less rightly telling him how to set about the writing of a novel. Hardy took the advice and exaggerated it in the thrills and surprising episodes which he heaped one on another in *Desperate Remedies*—a clever experiment in fiction, but not what we have come to think of as Hardy's.

Yet in the very next book, *Under the Greenwood Tree*, the real Hardy is present unmistakably. Already we strike the authentic note. No one could have done this book but Hardy, and, for what it is, it could scarcely have been done better. Here we have not yet reached the philosophy of Hardy; there is no sense of overwhelming destiny, no note of tragedy, no deep hint of the tears of things. It is not one of his greater books, yet I should profoundly regret it if he had not written it. It is a picture, an idyll, of Dorset country life as the author remembered it from his boyhood and before reflection had tinged it with bitterness. Here is Wessex—the Dorset country and people, the fir trees sobbing in the breeze, the ash hissing, the beeches rustling, the procession of villagers proceeding in the dark to the tranter's cottage, the rustic choir singing under Fancy Day's window, the dancing, the love-making that goes awry and ends gaily—all of this, the lovely raw material of rustic life as it might have been if no Spirit Sinister had left its mark, no 'viewless, voiceless Turner of the Wheel' had been discerned working havoc. It is the Garden of Eden before Adam fell; and if Fancy Day had ever so little of Eve's naughtiness, it was no more than enough to make her human. The scenes are real, the characters true to life; yet the book is not so much a novel as an idyll of English country life, a pastoral poem in prose.

The next book was to be a more ambitious essay in fiction, but far less satisfying. *A Pair of Blue Eyes* (published 1873) has received from many critics higher praise than I am able to give it. The total impression which this book leaves does not carry for me the unmistakable, unforgettable note of the essential Hardy. Several critics have divided Hardy's novels into three or four classes, and Hardy himself distinguished between kind and kind. Thus, Lionel Johnson, the earliest important critic of the novels, arranged them in three groups: the Tragic; the Idyllic; and the comic, ironic, satiric, romantic, extravagant. This division is well enough, but takes no account of a distinction which in my opinion is more important—a distinction of quality, between the books which spring from Hardy's essential genius and those which do not. The former come from the inner core of his creative imagination; the latter are fabricated. In the first he is possessed by his subject, in the second he is using his inventive talent to carry him as best it can through an ingenious story.

From first to last, Hardy, observant, percipient, sensitive and thoughtful as he was, was a person of great simplicity. There was something of the peasant in him which sophistication did not wholly eliminate. He grew up to know, as only an observant, percipient and sensitive person could have known, a world of a certain kind, filled with a certain life, human and natural—to know it in all its beauty, its contrariness, and its perplexing painfulness. That life, as he had known it from his childhood, he absorbed imaginatively, and it became the raw material of his art. He would never be at his best except when near to that life which he had thus absorbed, though he was to transcend it and put it in a vaster context. Even as a boy and young man it was being modified by his reading of English literature, the classics, and history, by his careful study of architecture, by his interest in pictures and in acting, his disturbing contacts with Darwin and Spencer and Schopenhauer, and his puzzled study of the Oxford Movement theologians and their opponents; and as a man he became more and more uneasy at innovations which were displacing rustic customs and social ideas at variance with the older codes of life; he found evils aggravated by the intolerant judgement of society, as if there were not enough that are beyond man's control and inherent in human life. Percipient, meditative, contemplative, he remained simple, a peasant burdened with knowledge which magnified the problems, heightened the significance of the emotions, and enlarged the objects of perception till they seemed to be co-existent with all the world and the infinite. The problems that were thus revealed were to become insoluble and almost unbearable, and the more so as men and women, the raw material of life, with primitive passions and developing consciousness, continuing their plodding existence, were converted into tragi-comic realities of the imagination. 'The business of the poet and novelist', he wrote in his Memoranda two days after he had written the last page of *The Mayor of Casterbridge*, 'is to show the sorriness underlying the grandest things, and the grandeur underlying the sorriest things.'

The people and the countryside of what he called Wessex, seen through the prism of a romantic imagination, provided for Hardy the archetypal forms of human existence; during the whole of his novel-writing period, the life, of this kind, that he portrayed became, when he was at his best, like the notes and chords in an orchestral composition moving from theme to theme as the motive dictated. He might be clumsy in individual passages, the plot might creak under the excessive use of coincidence, but the essence of the movement is there, the sureness of the motive unerring. Hardy is possessed by his subject. His assimilating and constructive imagination is engaged. And this is just as true in the case of a slight masterpiece such as *Under the Greenwood Tree* as in the grand tragedy of *The Return of the Native*, or *Tess*, or *The Mayor of Casterbridge*. But it was not always thus. At one moment, as we have seen, Hardy was diverted from his inclination by advice offered by the great Meredith. At another time, as his biographer tells, when 'he was committed by circumstances to novel-writing as a regular trade', he felt constrained to look about for material in social and fashionable life; his 'gloomy misgivings' on this score being confirmed in a talk with Miss Thackeray, who told him that 'a novelist must necessarily like society'. Moreover, the 'journeywork' of writing thrust upon him commitments to editors of magazines, demanding that he should write another book before his creative imagination was ready for the task. Under these circumstances it is easy to understand that he should have written a number of books which, though they would have been creditable to a lesser novelist, lack, each considered as a whole, the mark of the real Hardy. The sum-total of his work would not be much impoverished if we removed altogether *A Pair of Blue Eyes*, *The Hand of Ethelberta*, *A Laodicean* and *Two on a Tower*—books which were interspersed among the finest of his novels.

This is not to say that there are not many excellencies in these books, and passages in which the writer reveals his distinctive power. *A Pair of Blue Eyes* commands the reader's interest from beginning to end. The theme is that of a woman's inconstancy, one not likely to be dully treated by Hardy, who idealized the opposite quality, that of long-suffering constancy in love, in Tess, Giles Winterbourne, Marty South, Gabriel Oak, the Trumpet-Major. Hardy found the making of much tragedy in the possession or lack of that virtue. In *Jude the Obscure* passion, for Sue, began with 'the love of being loved'; in Elfride, in *A Pair of Blue Eyes*, it began in 'the love of admiration'. In retrospect there is the memory of a first entanglement, the young man whom she had kissed on the tomb; he had died. In the early part of this book she becomes engaged to the young architect, secretly, for he is of humble origin; runs away to be married, but does not marry. In the next phase she succumbs to the superior qualities of her lover's rather priggish friend. By a series of accidents the third lover discovers all that has happened, suspects more, and goes. Lovers number two and three travel together to Elfride's village on a train, and find that it also carries a hearse and her body; that she had married a fourth lover and died. Thus baldly outlined the story sounds melodramatic and absurd, and in fact it is not without these defects. Yet Elfride is well enough done to gain our sympathy and Knight to earn our dislike; the narrative is alive and often exciting, as in the episode on The Cliff without a Name; and though the scene is in Cornwall, and not in Hardy's more intimately known Dorset, there are passages of description which show that he had already intuitively discovered a way of conveying through the medium of words what a painter conveys in a picture, but by devices appropriate to the art of letters. Hardy knows that by writing you cannot 'paint' a scene; to attempt to do by successive words what a painter does by co-existent images in a picture is merely to bewilder the reader, as by a catalogue; he prefers to describe through action, to show things moving, breathing, appearing; to give us as much that can be *heard* as *seen*; to record the effect left on the mind of a spectator. Though we can find much finer passages in Hardy's other books, this power of literary description is exhibited many times in *A Pair of Blue Eyes*, as thus, when Stephen stood at the door of the church porch looking for Elfride:

> The faint sounds heard only accentuated the silence. The rising and falling of the sea, far away along the coast, was the most important. A minor sound was the scurr of a distant night-hawk. Among the minutest where all were minute were the light settlement of gossamer fragments floating in the air, a toad humbly labouring along through the grass near the entrance, the crackle of a dead leaf which a worm was endeavouring to pull into the earth, a waft of air, getting nearer and nearer, and expiring at his feet under the burden of a winged insect.

In such passages as that we have the authentic note that is Hardy's.

The Hand of Ethelberta is one of those books that I have spoken of as being 'fabricated'. When he wrote that, Hardy was taking Miss Thackeray's advice—he was entering society, describing a life which he could report but not build up through his own vision. It is incidentally interesting as affording an example of Hardy's consciousness of class distinction, discernible in greater or less degree in most of his novels.

A Laodicean is generally, and rightly, spoken of as the worst of his novels. Much of it was written when he was ill but under contract to provide chapters month by month for an editor. Hardy had doubtless intended to write a book illustrating the contrast between the ancient and the modern, the inherited and the acquired, the dignity of the old order and the indignity of modern progress. He produced in fact a crudely thrilling melodrama in which villainy, blackmail, eavesdropping and violence produce a succession of reversals of fortune ending happily in marriage. Hardy sufficiently described the book himself in one of his later Prefaces. '*A Laodicean* may perhaps help to while away an idle afternoon of the comfortable ones whose lines have fallen to them in pleasant places; above all, of that large and happy section of the reading public which has not yet reached ripeness of years.'

Two on a Tower is not very much better than *A Laodicean*, though the series of coincidences which thwart hero and heroine are less absurd. It concerns a love affair between a young man of peasant birth who is becoming a brilliant astronomer, and a lady of aristocratic family who has been deserted by her husband; and the love scenes take place on a lonely tower where the young man introduces Lady Constantine to the fixed stars. 'This slightly-built romance', wrote Hardy thirteen years later, 'was the outcome of a wish to set the emotional history of two infinitesimal lives against the stupendous background of the stellar universe.'

The books of which I have just been speaking may be considered as minor episodes in Hardy's work. Like his other and greater books they are love stories depending for their development on the external incidents of plot. Hardy firmly believed that a novel should tell a story, and with him the story always turned upon actual events in the lives of his persons. He spoke slightingly about Henry James's preoccupation with 'the minutiae of manners'. 'James's subjects are those one could be interested in at moments when there is nothing larger to think of.' What Hardy sought was an action exhibiting the simple, elemental emotions, such as had been chosen by the Greek tragedians and Shakespeare. In the lesser books, where his imagination was not fully engaged, the story is just a story, ingeniously contrived, whose incidents afford occasions for exhibiting individual characters; but the characters do not stand in symbolic relationship to a pattern of life. The poet in him asserted itself from time to time, but did not control the situation. He told his story with a sort of ingenuous fidelity to his task, and that was all. But when the grand moment came Hardy the poet-novelist took charge. The dividing-line between his greater work and his lesser is absolute. To the former belong unmistakably *Under the Greenwood Tree, Far From the Madding Crowd, The Return of the Native, The Trumpet-Major, The Mayor of Casterbridge, The Woodlanders, Tess of the D'Urbervilles* and *Jude the Obscure*.

Hardy had the mind of a poet. He was reading and writing poetry through all the years of his novel-writing, and he turned finally to poetry when he had said his say in the appropriate form of fiction and came to the grand summing-up. He had the imagination of Coleridge's creative poet who seeks to externalize all the world that he is aware of in terms of his understanding of it. That being so his art was from its nature progressive, revealing the successive stages of his discovery of life. No author's work reveals a clearer pattern, moving on stage by stage in the elucidation of life, not by argument or teaching, but by exhibiting life itself, human beings in action, driven by forces they do not understand. It begins with the simpler material of human life, men and women shown under stress of emotion, generally in a rustic setting. It ends with all history in time, all the universe in space, and the Kosmos which includes all space and time and the possible beyond. His real creative work shows a steady progression from perception of an individual to perception of the Universal. In the latter case I say *perception*, not *conception*, for even the Universal is individualized, and perceived through the eye of the artist.

Each of Hardy's finer novels may be taken as a projection of his state of awareness at a certain stage of his development; its material is the world which he felt to be real. The content of that world, when he wrote *Under the Greenwood Tree*, was that Wessex life of which I have spoken and all the memories of youth it included. It was still such that it could be presented idyllically, with the rhythmic pattern of a pastoral poem. If the course of true love is not quite smooth, it is only so little troubled as to make the smoothing pleasant. The village which is the scene of action stands for all the English villages whose life is cast in the traditional mould. But Hardy has moved on when he comes two years later to *Far From the Madding Crowd*. The country life is in essentials the same, though we see it on a larger scale. It is more consciously conceived as something which does not change, remaining 'ancient' when so much else is becoming 'modern'. 'In Weatherbury three or four score years were included in the mere present, and nothing less than a century set a mark on its face or tone. Five decades hardly modified the cut of a gaiter, the embroidering of a smock-frock, by the breadth of a hair. Ten generations failed to alter the turn of a single phrase.' The more important persons, with one exception, might have behaved as they do here a century or two ago; the exception being Bathsheba herself, the first example which Hardy gives us of a partly emancipated woman, who farms her own farm and demands equal status with the men when she goes to Casterbridge market. The story, as in most of Hardy's novels, is essentially a love story. It touches a deeper note which has the quality of tragedy, but the disturbance arises not, as we are to feel later, from any cruelty in the nature of things, but from the conflict between the characters, and their responses to impulse or to those accidents which play too frequent a part in all Hardy's plots. For Hardy, love is always treated as the major passion in life, and constancy in love is shown as the major virtue, accompanied by other excellences which it implies. Gabriel Oak stands side by side with John Loveday, Giles Winterbourne, Marty South, and the Reddleman, among the heroes and heroines whose love is proof against all shocks. Farmer Oak is slow, deliberate, moving with quiet energy. Though if occasion demanded he could 'do or think a thing with as mercurial a dash as can the man of towns... his special power, morally, physically, and mentally, was static, owing little or nothing to momentum'. When he looked at the sky he drew practical conclusions about the time and the weather, but 'being a man not without a frequent consciousness that there was some charm in this life he led, he stood still after looking at the sky as a useful instrument, and regarded it in an appreciative spirit, as a work of art supremely beautiful'. He does not hesitate to criticize Bathsheba when she has offended his sense of right, and can help her as none other can in moments of crisis, yet he has not that sort of masterfulness which would compel her to love him. He will not, like Farmer Boldwood, press his claims because she has flirted with him. He is not the man to plead where he is not wanted. And Bathsheba, for all her strength and good sense, proves to be at the mercy of her own impetuosity where the heart is involved, and falls all too easy a prey to the handsome, adventurous seducer, Troy—though, once again, it is an accident which plays its part in leading her to marry him. The story pursues its way rhythmically through incidents which stir the emotions of three men and a girl, amid the rustic events of sheep-shearing, stacking, marketing, in calm and in storm, to a running commentary of gossip from the chorus of workers. The ending is a compromise between that of tragedy and comedy. Gabriel marries Bathsheba, but not till his rivals have been tragically removed.

Far From the Madding Crowd established Hardy's reputation, but it was to be followed disappointingly by *The Hand of Ethelberta*, and that by a masterpiece, *The Return of the Native*. But first, a word about *The Trumpet-Major*, a novel which, in Hardy's natural development, might well have come before rather than just after *The Return of the Native*. We know from his Memoranda that in 1875, five years before *The Trumpet-Major* was published, three years before *The Return of the Native*, Hardy's mind was moving towards the theme which was to become that of *The Dynasts*. 'Mem:' he wrote at that time, 'a Ballad of the Hundred Days. Then another of Moscow. Others of earlier campaigns

—forming altogether an Iliad of Europe from 1789 to 1815.' And two years later he wrote, 'Consider a grand drama, based on the wars with Napoleon, or some one campaign (but not as Shakespeare's historical dramas). It might be called "Napoleon" or "Josephine", or by some other person's name.' But long before then Hardy had been deeply interested in the recollections of old persons whom he had known in childhood, who had been eye-witnesses of the events that occurred in Dorset when the invasion of England by Napoleon was daily expected. As a boy he had studied the 'casual relics' of the preparations for defence—'a heap of bricks and clods on a beacon-hill', 'worm-eaten shafts and iron heads of pikes', 'ridges on the down thrown up during the encampment, fragments of volunteer uniform, and other such lingering remains'. These discoveries profoundly affected the imagination of the young Hardy, and gave him an insight into the condition of England at the time of Trafalgar; and this early knowledge was to be extended later by close study of the history of the period. Already, before he wrote *The Trumpet-Major*, Hardy was imaginatively seeing the history of his native district in the larger perspective of England and Napoleon's Europe, just as so often in his stories of individuals living in a Wessex homestead we find the pressure of a wider humanity surging round and beyond. 'A certain provincialism of feeling is invaluable', he wrote in the very year of *The Trumpet-Major*. 'It is the essence of individuality, and is largely made up of that crude enthusiasm without which no great thoughts are thought, no great deeds done.'

And so it is with *The Trumpet-Major*. Though in a certain sense it is the story of love-affairs written in the spirit of light comedy, its lightness is that of the provincial scenes in *The Dynasts*—it is the relief to a vaster background of historic events; it is the village commentary on life the day before the battle. The slight love story will stand on its own merits, but it becomes something more when it is an interlude in a world-conflict. Not that Hardy presses upon us these sterner reflections. In this historical novel we are much nearer to *Under the Greenwood Tree* than to *Jude*. There is enough to entertain us in the succession of lively pictures which Hardy draws—the cavalry soldiers on their bulky grey chargers ascending the down and preparing the camp while the romantic Anne looks on from the miller's cottage, the excitement in the village, the party at the miller's, the behaviour of the solid John Loveday, the soldier, and his lively, mercurial brother, Bob, the King's visit to Budmouth, the false alarm when the beacon is lit, and the ups and downs of Bob's affections. There are touches of melodrama when the bully Festus has too many opportunities for playing the villain or when Matilda exceeds herself as the scarlet woman. But it is all part of the play—vigorous, zestful play—whose romance takes a deeper note when it describes the simple fidelity of John to his unattainable beloved and his unstable brother. Though not a major novel, this has its place in the sequence of Hardy's genuine works.

The five greater novels, which it remains to consider, are all tragedy, tragedy on the grand scale. They are all of them love stories, as before, but the men and women who suffer this passion in its extremity, individual as they are, become also representatives of the human race; and we are to see them through Hardy's eyes, as Aeschylus saw Prometheus chained to a rock, against a vast background of nature, the victim of 'the President of the Immortals'. The magnificent opening pages of *The Return of the Native*, showing in the description of Egdon Heath what sort of a place it was in which the persons were to suffer, creates an impression of Nature more sombre than we have had before, indeed a Nature which appeared to share the sufferings of men. 'Fair prospects wed happily with fair times; but alas, if times be not fair . . . Haggard Egdon appealed to a subtler and scarcer instinct, to a more recently learnt emotion . . . wearing a sombreness distasteful to our race when it was young.' 'The storm was its lover, and the wind its friend.' It could become 'the home of strange phantoms'. 'Like man, slighted and enduring', it was 'colossal and mysterious in its swarthy monotony'. In *The Woodlanders*, too, though there are some gentler pictures, 'the bleared white visage of a sunless winter day emerged like a dead-born child', and in the wood we observe 'the Unfulfilled Intention, which makes life what it is', working havoc underground—'the leaf was deformed, the curve was crippled, the taper was interrupted; the lichen ate the vigour of the stalk and the ivy slowly strangled to death the promising sapling'. Though Nature assumes a far sweeter aspect at Talbothays during those months when Tess and Clare were working among the cows and the meadows, the sweetness of it becomes as a foil to the horrors which are to follow.

Hardy peoples this alternately lovely and sinister world with men and women, the more ordinary of whom play the chorus, and others, the exceptional ones, some capable of intense emotion, others, in a worse plight, equally emotional but also acutely conscious and self-conscious, feeling in themselves what Tess 'was expressing in her own native phrases—assisted a little by her Sixth Standard training—feelings which might almost have been called those of the age—the ache of modernism'. In *The Return of the Native* Clym Yeobright's face reflected 'the view of life as a thing to be put up with, replacing that zest for existence which was so intense in early civilizations'. Henchard in *The Mayor of Casterbridge* perceives more simply but passionately. The shape of his ideas in time of affliction was simply 'a moody "I am to suffer, I perceive"'; his superstitious nature led to the grim conclusion that his misfortunes were due to 'some sinister intelligence bent on punishing him'. In *Jude the Obscure* the percipience of the new type of human being reaches an extremity where it is unbearable. Even as a boy Jude showed that he was 'the sort of man who was born to ache'; he was at moments 'seized with a sort of shuddering'. As a man he was a victim of 'the modern vice of unrest'. Sue the ethereal, the fine-nerved, the idealist, had the same sensitiveness, and became almost masochistic in her love of suffering. Hardy pursues the theme to a point where it becomes almost horrible in reproducing the affliction of the parents in their children. 'I ought not to be born, ought I?' says Little Father Time, working himself up to the mood which ends in the hanging of himself and his baby brother and sister. 'The doctor', it is reported, 'says there are such boys springing up amongst us—boys of a sort unknown in the last generation. . . . It is the beginning of the coming universal wish not to live'.

These five books are not to be taken as a statement of Hardy's philosophy. But in giving body to human life as this meditative man finds it a pattern appears, a pattern in accordance with which human nature manifests itself; the pattern yields a philosophy, imposed on Hardy by his intuitive reading of experience. There emerges a sort of theory of society into which the facts, as he sees them, fit; it widens into nothing less than a view of the universe. Already in *The Return of the Native* we are faced with the problem of a young man of bucolic origin moving too quickly to intellectual and sophisticated aims, reaching a condition of unbalance between the two elements in himself. In *The Mayor of Casterbridge* we have in Lucetta the half-emancipated woman—'I'll love whom I choose', though, the old superstition still strong in her, she shrinks and withers to her death before the terrors of the skimmity-ride. In *The Woodlanders* we are introduced to the deficiencies of the divorce laws; in *Tess* to the cruelty of public opinion towards those who have offended against its decrees; and in *Jude* Sue Bridehead, so clear-sighted in vision, though so unreasonable in action, makes her explicit protest against 'the social moulds civilization fits us into'; and asks whether a marriage ceremony is a religious thing, or 'only a sordid contract, based on material convenience in householding, rating, and taxing, and the inheritance of land and money by children'. 'When people of a later age look back upon the barbarous customs and superstition of the times that we have the unhappiness to live in, what *will* they say!' she exclaims. And before then even Jude, with his more conventional views, finding his life ruined by marriage with the coarse, dissolute Arabella, had reflected on the fundamental error of 'having based a permanent contract on a temporary feeling'.

In these his subtlest and most tragic books we have a searching criticism of modern life and finally of all life. We have still the chorus of ordinary men and women, with rustic minds not yet unhinged, accepting life and judging it, gaily or sadly, in accordance with the older standards. But in the forefront we have others, born in the same milieu, who have come to put everything to the question; who have acquired the self-consciousness which is the distinctive characteristic of modern man; who question the fundamentals of the society we live in, the rightness of social conventions, the sanctity of the marriage contract, the goodness of a progress and a civilization which bring so much misery to man, and finally, the benevolence or the omnipotence of the Power that rules the Universe. Clym Yeobright saw 'the whole creation groaning and travailing in pain'. Henchard feared 'some sinister intelligence'. Tess supposed that we live on a star that is 'a blighted one'; she questioned the 'use of learning', though 'I shouldn't mind learning why— why the sun do shine on the just and the unjust alike. . . . But that's what books will not tell me.' Sue Fawley had once imagined that 'the world resembled a stanza or melody composed in a dream', but her fully awakened intelligence concluded that 'the First Cause worked automatically like a somnambulist, and not reflectively like a sage'. 'All the ancient wrath of the Power above us has been vented upon us, His poor creatures, and we must submit.' Sue comes near to expressing the developed cosmology of *The Dynasts*. The characters, more sinned against than sinning, are those of human beings set in a framework of universal Destiny.

Hardy did not set out to give us a pessimistic philosophy. He did set out to show how certain persons, selected because they were interesting, having certain characters, would behave under certain circumstances, arbitrarily conceived, but not impossible. In bringing them to disaster he is prone to weight the chances against their prosperity by too many coincidences; his frequent use of the unlucky accident is a blemish in nearly all of his plots—the accident that Giles Winterbourne should fail to notice the writing which Grace chalked on his wall, or that grim mishap in *The Return of the Native* which prevents the opening of the door, when Clym's mother had made her dreary journey over the heath to be reconciled with her son and his wife: ' 'Tis too much, Clym. How can he bear to do it! He is at home; and yet he lets her shut the door against me!' Hope turns to gloom and disaster.

It has been claimed, and I think rightly, that Hardy has elevated the function of the novel, and succeeded in placing it among the greatest of the literary art forms. He has told in each case a tale, and in that respect it stands on the merits proper to a tale. Each also contains characters which are faithfully and subtly exhibited. But that is not all. The action is significant. It moves according to a pattern which is part of the pattern of all life, and so yields an account of the world and the universe we live in. This seen tract of life unfolded before our eyes springs from Hardy's vision of life as a whole; it is nothing less than his conception of the Universe expressing itself at given moments of time and in a given place, and the time and even the place itself participate in his cosmic conception. Just as Shakespeare calls upon the whole of his imagination when he makes a Macbeth or a Lear, and Milton in his quite different way when he presents the Archangels at War, so does Hardy when he shows Mrs. Yeobright striving to overcome her prejudices or Michael Henchard proceeding headlong to a doom brought down on him by his own arrogance and obstinacy, or poor Tess harassed and killed by the avenging Furies of conventional opinion.

The tragedy, however, does not always follow the Aristotelean rules. A good plot (in spite of the coincidences);

characters, serious and deserving of our attention; action, calling forth pity and fear; all of these are present. But Hardy sometimes violates the rule which forbade the shocking spectacle of a virtuous person brought through no fault of his own from prosperity to adversity. In *Jude the Obscure* Hardy goes to extremes in showing men and women pursued relentlessly by a cruel 'Universe' through no fault of their own. This novel, I think, immense as it is in dissecting the problems of Jude and Sue Fawley, and describing their relations with each other, does leave at the end a sense of horror which is incompatible with the highest art. But in this case alone. In *The Return of the Native* the two characters who matter are Clym and his mother, Mrs. Yeobright; the tragedy is brought about by the error of Clym, who misconceives his mission in life, and above all by Mrs. Yeobright, whose prejudice and obstinacy are not atoned for by her gestures of forgiveness. In *The Mayor of Casterbridge* it is the recklessness, the pride, the unforgiving obstinacy of Henchard's nature which cause his downfall. His tragedy, like Lear's, is the tragedy of his own soul.

There is no comparable fault or error in the protagonists of *The Woodlanders* or *Tess*; yet we are not disgusted, unless it be by the violence with which Tess's life is ended. If in these cases we are not shocked, but on the contrary are profoundly moved by the behaviour of the persons and the sublimity of the scene, I think we shall discover that that is because the disaster is not complete. Destiny may seem pitiless and cruel, but the nobility of the characters in facing it with courage and sympathy towards one another evokes a compensating admiration. In *The Woodlanders* the devotion of Giles to Grace is unfailing, and at the end the tragedy of his death is softened by the triumph of the sacrifice of himself for her sake, and beautified by the unfailing and apparently unrewarded love of Marty South. Marty's patient love, serenely in the background throughout the story, breathed only to the young larches, is immortalized in the book's silences and in the lyrical whispered cry with which it ends.

And even in *Tess*, when ' "Justice" was done, and the President of the Immortals, in Aeschylean phrase, had ended his sport with Tess', and had shown the last of her, so grimly, on the gallows, the penultimate scene had its compensation. It brought happiness—Tess called it happiness—in the final reunion and understanding between herself and Clare. When the pursuers at last find them at Stonehenge, 'It is as it should be', she murmured. 'Angel, I am almost glad—yes, glad! This happiness could not have lasted. It was too much.' She faces the end with her habitual courage. ' "I am ready", she said quietly.'

Hardy is pessimistic about the governance of the Universe, but not about human beings. In his lesser books there are villains playing their melodramatic parts, but in his greater novels there are no villains. There are weak, and volatile, and selfish people, like Wildeve or Fitzpiers; but they are not simply scoundrels. There can be a coarse, unscrupulous creature, like Arabella, but even she is not wholly bad. The chorus of ordinary men and women are full of good humour and the milk of human kindness. The heroes and heroines have noble and lovable qualities; they stand in sublime contrast to the supreme Powers. Giles Winterbourne, 'born and bred among the orchards', who 'looked and smelt like Autumn's very brother', is endowed with the qualities which Christians have allotted to the saints. And with what wonderful words does Mrs. Cuxsom reveal both herself and the dead woman of whom she speaks.

> 'And she was as white as marble-stone. And likewise such a thoughtful woman, too—ah, poor soul—that a' minded every little thing that wanted tending. "Yes," says she, "when I'm gone, and my last breath's blowed, look in the top drawer o' the chest in the back room by the window, and you'll find all my coffin clothes; a piece of flannel—that's to put under me, and the little piece is to put under my head; and my new stockings for my feet—they are folded alongside, and all my other things. And there's four ounce pennies, the heaviest I could find, a-tied up in bits of linen, for weights—two for my right eye and two for my left", she said. "And when you've

used 'em and my eyes don't open no more, bury the pennies, good souls, and don't ye go spending 'em, for I shouldn't like it. And open the windows as soon as I am carried out, and make it as cheerful as you can for Elizabeth-Jane".'

The grimly comic is not lacking when she tells how Christopher Coney dug up and spent the pennies. The passage ends with one of those lyrical sayings which abound in the prose of this poet.

'Well, poor soul, she's helpless to hinder that or anything else now', answered Mother Cuxsom. 'And all her shining keys will be took from her, and her cupboards opened; and little things a' didn't wish seen, anybody will see; and her wishes and ways will all be as nothing.'

Hardy, a meditative poet, gave to the novel a sublimity to which in his own country it had not attained before. His procedure is architectural. Out of all the elements in life which he knows he builds up, through a series of novels, a whole which embraces the kind of men and women he has observed, the beautiful English country they have lived in, the memory of the past which has haunted them, and the whole panorama of life and death, filled with love and jealousy, ambition, fear, and unfulfilled ideals. His style moves for the most part slowly and cumbrously, sometimes awkwardly, like Gabriel Oak's walk; he has no scholarly fastidiousness of language; yet in moments of excitement or tension or deep emotion it breaks through its impediments, becoming now vivacious, now brilliant, now lovely in its still depths. But for the most part the effects are cumulative; he assembles piece by piece the elements which go to the making of a vast panorama.

I have said that Hardy's art was progressive, revealing the successive stages in his discovery of life. When he had written *Jude* he probably felt that he had said all that he had to say in novel form. The torrent of invective which that book drew down upon him from the critics was an experience which, he said seventeen years later, completely cured him of further interest in novel writing. But that can scarcely be the whole or even the main reason for his abandoning prose fiction. He had always known himself to be a poet, and he was a poet whether he wrote in prose or verse; and he was now free to follow his bent. But there were overwhelming reasons, inherent in his own development, why he should turn from novels to the epic drama of *The Dynasts*. He had spent twenty-five years in the effort to state life in terms of life; the novels were an objective expression of the raw material of experience; his gradual discovery of what life consists of led to those novels; experience, intuition, meditation, gave birth to those tracts of human experience there exposed; and already before he had done with them, they were revealing themselves in a wider context, that of the history of mankind and man's place in the Universe. It remained for him to state his conclusions—not philosophically, for his mind worked imaginatively, but in a poem. *The Dynasts* is the summing-up of all that he has done before.

'Ay; begin small, and so lead up to the greater. It is a sound dramatic principle.' Thus the Spirit Sinister in *The Dynasts*, in reply to the Spirit of the Years, who had called the attention of the assembled Spirits to some human beings travelling in a stage-coach over a ridge in Wessex, in March 1905. Hardy's own literary work had proceeded in this way, beginning small with light poems and *Under the Greenwood Tree*, gaining volume and depth as the novels progressed, and culminating in his great Epic Drama. He had for many years been preparing himself for the subject he here treats, 'the Great Historical Calamity, or Clash of Peoples', in the Napoleonic wars; for the use of verse as a literary medium; and for a cosmological survey of the human race. I have already alluded to his studies of the Napoleonic wars, which he used in the small beginnings of *The Trumpet-Major*, and of his growing interest in the scheme of an Epic of Napoleon. It was natural that he should link this up with his studies of individual human beings whom he had observed tragically out of harmony with the 'social moulds' of modern life, and as the victims of a Fate which appeared to dog them senselessly and pitilessly.

In form *The Dynasts* is both Epic and Drama. It uses both narrative and dialogue, mainly in verse, but partly in prose. Its subject in the narrower sense is that of the Napoleonic wars from 1805 to 1815 (followed in strict accord with historic evidence) with special reference to the part played by England in the European conflict. There are many scores of persons, conspicuous among them Napoleon, Pitt, Nelson, George III, Villeneuve, the Emperors Francis and Alexander, the Empress Josephine, Lady Hester Stanhope, and many Admirals, Marshals, politicians, priests, Court ladies, and humble sailors, soldiers, burgesses, beacon-watchers, and rustics, seen and heard on the continent of Europe or in England or at sea. Regarded as historic epic the work presents a colossal, and I believe accurate, historic pageant of the leaders and common people of Europe in the greatest human conflict prior to the recent world wars. But it is much more than that; it follows the classic examples of Homer's *Iliad* and Milton's *Paradise Lost* in introducing extra-terrestrial Powers, and allotting to them an integral part in the action. But there are significant differences, corresponding to the differences in thought, which put a gulf between Hardy and the poets of less sceptical ages. The gods in Homer are like men, and intervene in their affairs; the Archangels of Milton are also anthropomorphically conceived, and intervene, benevolently or malignly, in the affairs of man. But the Immanent Will of *The Dynasts* from the nature of Its being cannot appear at all as a person or a speaker. As for the Spirits—the Ancient Spirit and Chorus of the Years, the Spirit and Chorus of the Pities, the Shade of the Earth, the Spirits Sinister and Ironic with their Choruses, and the Rumours, Spirit-Messengers and Recording Angels—they do not, with two or three exceptions, interfere at all in the sphere of men; they are observers, recorders, commentators. We are to discover that it is not we, human beings, who are primarily the audience, the spectators, of the drama. The play is played to the Spirits; it is they who watch it, they who judge it, and express their sympathy or indifference. The vast panoramic struggle is thrown as it were on a terrific screen which embraces the whole of Europe, and seen through the eyes of non-human Intelligences. Behind all is the Immanent Will and Its designs.

> It works unconsciously, as heretofore,
> Eternal artistries in Circumstance,
> Whose patterns, wrought by rapt aesthetic rote,
> Seem in themselves Its single listless aim,
> And not their consequence.

'In the Foretime', adds the Spirit of the Years,

> Nothing appears of shape to indicate
> That cognizance has marshalled things terrene,
> Or will (such is my thinking) in my span.
> Rather they show that, like a knitter drowsed,
> Whose fingers ply in skilled unmindfulness,
> The Will has woven with an absent heed
> Since life first was; and ever will so weave.

The Spirit of the Years, aloof and passionless, presides among the Spirits as the play goes on before them; the Pities, as Hardy pointed out, approximate to what Schlegel called 'the Universal Sympathy of human nature—the Spectator idealized', of the Greek Chorus. The speeches of the Spirits constitute a sublime play beyond the play; they are in strong, rhythmic, sonorous verse appropriate to their dignity, the vocabulary strangely compounded of long Latin words and terse, pithy Anglo-Saxon words such as

> You'll mark the twitchings of this Bonaparte
> As he with other figures foots his reel,
> Until he twitch him into his lonely grave.

The stage descriptions embrace all Europe and the scene gives us people in millions. 'The nether sky opens, and

Europe is disclosed as a prone and emaciated figure, the Alps shaping like a backbone, and the branching mountain-chains like ribs, the peninsula plateau of Spain forming a head....' 'The peoples, distressed by events which they did not cause, are seen writhing, crawling, heaving, and vibrating in their various cities and nationalities.' What a fore-glimpse, in 1903, of the world wars to follow, as seen from the onlooker's stall.

The human play is methodically pursued, with varying power. Some of the 'small' things are among the best, where Hardy, in appropriate prose, writes of his Wessex folk, talking with their native humour in the vernacular; or Wessex soldiers, fighting in Spain, recalling their old loves at home; or French soldiers, in their distracted retreat from Moscow. His love of the gruesome comes out in the *Mad Soldier's Song* (sung in the retreat):

> What can we wish for more?
> Thanks to the frost and flood
> We are grinning crones—thin bags of bones
> Who once were flesh and blood.
> So foolish life adieu
> And ingrate leader too.
> —Ah, but we loved you true!
> Yet—he-he-he! and ho-ho-ho!—
> We'll never return to you.

To meet the ends of an action which covers so wide a field, in so many representative scenes, the language varies in power and dignity. The verse is always vigorous, but not always at a high level of poetry. But who before has attempted in verse the task of reporting a Parliamentary debate? Even so Pitt in one of his speeches talks in successful verse almost as Churchill has talked in prose.

> The strange fatality that haunts the times
> Wherein our lot is cast, has no example.
> Times are they fraught with peril, trouble, gloom;
> We have to mark their lourings, and to face them.

THOMAS HARDY 33

The speeches of Napoleon are usually rhetorical, but there is vivacity and force in the rhetoric. The strategists, statesmen, courtiers, talk in character. The action proceeds from scene to scene with swiftness and unfailing energy, and we can read on as we would read a story, eager to follow the thrilling narrative, and stirred by the dark adventures and bold exhibitions of character. Sometimes—even on the battlefield of Waterloo—we are gripped by the poetic sense of the continuing life of the earth—the earth that Hardy knows in Wessex—but grimly threatened by the human conflict.

> Yea, the coneys are scared by the thud of hoofs,
> And their white scuts flash at their vanishing heels,
> And swallows abandon the hamlet-roofs.

It is a singular fact that in this drama of a European war Hardy should so write that we can never forget that Wessex coast and the people who live in the Wessex villages. Though Hardy is a good world-citizen, and once said that the sentiment of *Foreignness* should 'attach only to other planets and their inhabitants, if any', we feel none the less that he is stirred by English patriotism, that he admires the patriotic sentiments which Pitt expresses, and loves the innate and ineradicable patriotism—provincialism, if you like—of the English countryman. Though he is completely objective in his treatment of friends and enemies of the English, and rejects nationalism in his sympathy and in his pity for human beings, none the less the pulse of the poet seems to beat a little faster when he exhibits the reflections of a Pitt, the emotions of a Nelson, or the sentiment and humour of the English rustic. He has not set himself to praise England as Virgil in the *Æneid* sang the praises of Rome; none the less there emerges in the course of the Epic a sort of personality which is that of the English people, with qualities very dear to the poet, compounded of good and bad, serious and comic, but, in the sum, both noble and lovable. But these qualities are also those of the human race. Much of the tragic irony lies in this contrast between the essential goodness and kindliness of human beings and the blank indifference, the unkindness, of the irresistible Universe. The Spirit of the Pities recalls the words of Sophocles, who 'dubbed the Will "the gods"'.

Truly said he,
'Such gross injustice to their own creation
Burdens the time with mournfulness for us,
And for themselves with shame'.

The Dynasts is a large-scale action planned to project the situation of the whole human race, which consists of individuals possessing a sense of justice and noble aspirations, frustrated, as it seems to them, by an irresistible and indifferent Destiny. The whole is an imaginative picture, not a set of dogmas; but it yields the conclusion which arises irresistibly from those samples of life which he has given in the novels.

The novels are as full of poetry as is this Epic. The Epic itself contains many prose passages, and some of the speeches written in verse would have been equally, sometimes more, satisfactory in prose. He traverses the low ground of less distinguished speech and high ground where his verse becomes equal to the strain, and exhibits extreme vigour and sometimes a rare and forceful imagery which touches the higher peaks of poetry. He is not a fastidious writer with sure touch in the use of words, and yet in a few passages the words could not be bettered—that occurs when he is fully possessed by the emotional content of his theme and the words seem to pour from him irresistibly in their own right.

The Dynasts is the indispensable culmination of his work. It is as necessary as *War and Peace* is to Tolstoy, combining, as that book does, the individual and the universal. The private tragedies which in Tolstoy were interwoven with the world catastrophe are more subtly treated by the Russian and more poignant; Tolstoy's individuals are more individual, more alive. But all this, the human side of life,

THOMAS HARDY 35

had already been presented by Hardy in his novels, with less aloofness, but with consummate power. *The Dynasts* has an advantage over *War and Peace* in its unity and orchestration. It is the finale of the great body of work which had begun in his youth, matured in his middle age, and concludes itself here. He had surpassed any other English novelist in using the novel as an artistic vehicle for projecting life in its totality, realistically, emotionally, meditatively; in doing with it what hitherto only poetry had done, and fitting it into a structure sublimely conceived, and capable of summary in a final work which in form as well as substance was poetic.

His verse, other than *The Dynasts*, is no unimportant part of his work. Even the slighter pieces of his earlier years, and the meditative poems of his middle period—ballads which were short stories in verse, recollections of episodes remembered, reflections on the Immanent Will—help to fill in the grand structure, as the decorations in a cathedral add to its beauty and complete our awareness of the spirit that made it. Many of the poems of his old age are the best of all his short pieces, showing increased skill in versification, and originality in the use of expressive words; they have the gravity and the high reflectiveness of the experienced adult, and this combined with intensity of emotion.

To the last his mind and imagination were straining to search the mysteries of Nature, the Wessex people, England, and 'the full-starred heavens'.

> If, when hearing that I have been stilled at last, they stand at the door,
> Watching the full-starred heavens that winter sees,
> Will this thought rise on those who will meet my face no more,
> 'He was one who had an eye for such mysteries?'

THOMAS HARDY

A Select Bibliography

(Place of publication London, unless stated otherwise)

Bibliographies:

A DESCRIPTIVE CATALOGUE OF THE GROLIER CLUB CENTENARY EXHIBITION.
Ed. Carrole Wilson. Waterville, Maine (1940).

THE FIRST HUNDRED YEARS OF THOMAS HARDY (1840–1940).
A Centenary Bibliography of Hardiana, by C. J. Weber. Waterville, Maine (1942). Based on the extensive collection of books, etc., by and about Hardy at Colby College, Waterville, Maine.

THOMAS HARDY: A BIBLIOGRAPHICAL STUDY, by R. L. Purdy (1954).

Collected Editions:

WORKS IN PROSE AND VERSE (Thomas Hardy's Works). 18 vols. (1895–1913).

WORKS IN PROSE AND VERSE (Pocket Edition). 25 vols. (1906–19).

WORKS IN PROSE AND VERSE (Wessex Edition). 23 vols. (1912–13).

WORKS IN PROSE AND VERSE (Mellstock Edition). 37 vols. (1919–20).

COLLECTED POEMS. 2 vols. (1919; 1928).
Vol. I: *Poems*. Vol. II: *The Dynasts*.
The second (1923) and subsequent editions, in one volume, do not include *The Dynasts*. The first one-volume edition of *The Dynasts* was published in 1910 and there is a De Luxe edition in 3 vols. (1927).

COLLECTED SHORT STORIES (1928).

THE NOVELS (Library Edition) (1949 in progress).

SELECTED POEMS. Edited by G. M. Young (1940).

Separate Works:

DESPERATE REMEDIES. 3 vols. (1871). *Novel.*
First published anonymously.

38   A SELECT BIBLIOGRAPHY

UNDER THE GREENWOOD TREE. A Rural Painting of the Dutch School.
2 vols. (1872). *Novel.*
First published anonymously. 'A New Edition with a Portrait of
the Author and Fifteen Illustrations' (by Thomas Hardy) was published in 1891.

A PAIR OF BLUE EYES. A Novel. 3 vols. (1873). *Novel.*

FAR FROM THE MADDING CROWD. 2 vols. (1874). *Novel.*

THE HAND OF ETHELBERTA. A comedy in Chapters. 2 vols. (1876). *Novel.*

THE RETURN OF THE NATIVE. 3 vols. (1878). *Novel.*

THE TRUMPET-MAJOR. A Tale. 3 vols. (1880). *Novel.*

A LAODICEAN, or The Castle of the De Stancys. A Story of To-day.
3 vols. (1881). *Novel.*

TWO ON A TOWER. A Romance. 3 vols. (1882). *Novel.*

THE DORSET FARM LABOURER PAST AND PRESENT. Dorchester (1884).
Essay.

THE ROMANTIC ADVENTURES OF A MILKMAID. New York (1884). *Short
Story.*

THE MAYOR OF CASTERBRIDGE: The Life and Death of a Man of
Character. 2 vols. (1886). *Novel.*

THE WOODLANDERS. 3 vols. (1887). *Novel.*

WESSEX TALES: Strange, Lively and Commonplace. 2 vols. (1888).
Short Stories.

TESS OF THE D'URBERVILLES: A Pure Woman faithfully Presented.
3 vols. (1891). *Novel.*

A GROUP OF NOBLE DAMES (1891). *Short Stories.*

THE THREE WAYFARERS. A Pastoral Play in One Act. New York (1893).
Drama.
A dramatization of the short story 'The Three Strangers'.

LIFE'S LITTLE IRONIES. A Set of Tales with some Colloquial Sketches
entitled 'A Few Crusted Characters' (1894).
Includes 'The Melancholy Huzzar', first printed in *Three Notable
Stories* (1890); and 'To Please this Wife', first printed in *Stories from
'Black and White'*. (1893).

A SELECT BIBLIOGRAPHY   39

JUDE THE OBSCURE (1896). *Novel.*

THE SPECTRE OF THE REAL. *Short Story.*
In collaboration with F. Henniker. Published in *In Scarlet and Grey*
by F. Henniker (1896).

THE WELL-BELOVED. A Sketch of a Temperament (1897). *Novel.*

WESSEX POEMS and other Verses (1898). *Verse.*
With 30 illustrations by Thomas Hardy.

POEMS OF THE PAST AND THE PRESENT (1901). *Verse.*

THE DYNASTS. A Drama of the Napoleonic Wars. 3 parts (1903–4,
1906, 1908). *Verse Drama.*

TIME'S LAUGHING-STOCKS AND OTHER VERSES (1909). *Verse.*

A CHANGED MAN, THE WAITING SUPPER, AND OTHER TALES (1913). *Short
Stories.*
All these stories had previously been published in magazines, etc.

SATIRES OF CIRCUMSTANCE. Lyrics and Reveries (1914). *Verse.*

MOMENTS OF VISION, and Miscellaneous Verses (1917). *Verse.*

LATE LYRICS AND EARLIER. With Many Other Verses (1922). *Verse.*

THE FAMOUS TRAGEDY OF THE QUEEN OF CORNWALL AT TINTAGEL IN
LYONNESS (1923). *Verse Drama.*

HUMAN SHOWS, FAR PHANTASIES. SONGS AND TRIFLES (1925). *Verse.*

LIFE AND ART. New York (1925). *Essays and Letters.*
A Collection of essays, notes, and letters, not previously printed in
book form. Edited with an introduction by E. Brennecke.

WINTER WORDS, in Various Moods and Metres (1928). *Verse.*

OLD MRS. CHUNDLE. New York (1929). *Short Story.*
Not in the Collected Short Stories.

AN INDISCRETION IN THE LIFE OF AN HEIRESS (1935). *Short Novel.*
This adaptation by the author of his first novel *The Poor Man and
the Lady* was privately printed for Mrs. Hardy (1934); first published separately Baltimore, Maryland (1935) with an introduction
by C. J. Weber.

40 A SELECT BIBLIOGRAPHY

THE INTRUDER. Fairfield, Maine (1938). *Short Story.*
Not in the Collected Short Stories.

REVENGE IS SWEET: Two Short Stories. Waterville, Maine (1940). *Short Stories.*
This limited edition contains 'Destiny and a Blue Cloak' and 'The Doctor's Legend' previously unpublished in book form.

MAUMBURY RING. Waterville, Maine (1942). *Essay.*
Not published elsewhere.

OUR EXPLOITS AT WEST POLEY (1952). *Story.*

NOTEBOOKS AND SOME LETTERS, edited by E. Hardy (1955).

Some Critical and Biographical Studies:

THE ART OF THOMAS HARDY, by L. Johnson (1894; 1923 with supplementary material).
The 1923 edition contains a bibliography by J. Lane of first editions to 1922.

THE HARDY COUNTRY. Literary Landmarks of the Wessex Novels, by C. G. Harper (1904; 1925).

A THOMAS HARDY DICTIONARY, by F. O. Saxelby (1911).

THOMAS HARDY, by L. Abercrombie (1912).

THOMAS HARDY, by H. Child (1916).

THOMAS HARDY; A Study of the Wessex Novels, by H. C. Duffin. Manchester (1916; 3rd edition 1937).

THE TECHNIQUE OF THOMAS HARDY, by J. W. Beach (1922).

THOMAS HARDY'S UNIVERSE. A Study of a Poet's Mind, by E. Brennecke (1924).
See also the same author's *Life of Thomas Hardy*, 1925.

THE WESSEX NOVELS, by R. Williams (1924).

CHARACTER AND ENVIRONMENT IN THE NOVELS OF THOMAS HARDY, by H. B. Grimsditch (1925).

A STUDY OF THOMAS HARDY, by A. Symons (1927).

THOMAS HARDY AND HIS PHILOSOPHY, by P. Braybrooke (1928).

A SELECT BIBLIOGRAPHY 41

TALKS WITH THOMAS HARDY AT MAX GATE 1920–1922, by V. H. G. Collins (1928).

LE COUPLE HUMAIN DANS L'OEUVRE DE THOMAS HARDY, par. P. d'Exideuil, Paris (1928).
English translation from revised text by F. W. Crosse, with an introduction by H. Ellis [1930]. The French edition contains a list of French translations of Hardy's works.

THE EARLY LIFE OF THOMAS HARDY, 1840–1891, by F. E. Hardy (1928).

THE LATER YEARS OF THOMAS HARDY, 1892–1928, by F. E. Hardy (1930).
This work and the previous one by Hardy's widow, together comprise the standard biography of Hardy.

THOMAS HARDY. A Critical Study, by A. S. MacDowell (1931).

THOMAS HARDY, by W. R. Rutland. Oxford (1938).

THE DYNASTS AND THE POST-WAR AGE IN POETRY, by A. C. Chakravarty (1938).

HARDY OF WESSEX. His Life and Literary Career, by C. J. Weber. New York (1940).

THOMAS HARDY, by E. Blunden (1941).
In the English Men of Letters Series.

HARDY THE NOVELIST; an Essay in Criticism, by Lord David Cecil (1943).
The Clark Lectures at Cambridge (1942).

MY CHAT WITH THOMAS HARDY, by C. Clemens. Introduction by C. J. Weber (1944).

THE LYRICAL POETRY OF THOMAS HARDY, by C. M. Bowra. Nottingham (1946).
The Byron Lecture for 1946.

THE POETRY OF THOMAS HARDY, by J. G. Southworth. New York (1947).

ON A DARKLING PLAIN. The Art and Thought of Thomas Hardy, by H. C. Webster. Chicago (1947).

THOMAS HARDY: The Novels and Stories, by A. J. Guerard (1949).

A SELECT BIBLIOGRAPHY

THOMAS HARDY, by D. Hawkins (1950).
Although the edition bears this date, publication was in the following year.

FIFTY YEARS OF ENGLISH LITERATURE, 1900–1950, by R. A. Scott-James (1951).
Contains an assessment of Hardy as a lyric poet. See also this author's *Modernism and Romance* (1908).

THE POETRY OF THOMAS HARDY, by C. Day Lewis (1951).
A Lecture delivered before the British Academy, June 1951, and published in their *Proceedings*.

THOMAS HARDY, by R. A. S. James (1951).

THOMAS HARDY, by M. D. Brown (1954).

THOMAS HARDY. A critical biography by E. Hardy (1954).

Messrs. Macmillan publish Thomas Hardy's works in the Library Edition, the Pocket Edition, and the Scholars Library. They also publish his Collected Poems in one volume.

INDEX OF SHORT STORIES

(The title in brackets refers to the volumes in which the story appears)

Absent-Mindedness in a Parish Choir (*Life's Little Ironies*)

Alicia's Diary (*A Changed Man*)

Andrey Satchel and the Parson and Clerk (*Life's Little Ironies*)

Anna, Lady Baxby (*A Group of Noble Dames*)

Barbara of the House of Grebe (*A Group of Noble Dames*)

Changed Man, A (*A Changed Man*)

Committee-Man of 'The Terror', A (*A Changed Man*)

Distracted Preacher, The (*Wessex Tales*)

Duchess of Hamptonshire, The (*A Group of Noble Dames*)

Duke's Reappearance, The (*A Changed Man*)

Enter a Dragoon (*A Changed Man*)

Fellow-Townsmen (*Wessex Tales*)

Few Crusted Characters, A (*Life's Little Ironies*)

Fiddler of the Reels, The (*Life's Little Ironies*)

First Countess of Wessex, The (*A Group of Noble Dames*)

For Conscience' Sake (*Life's Little Ironies*)

Grave by the Handpost, The (*A Changed Man*)

History of the Hardcomes, The (*Life's Little Ironies*)

Honourable Laura, The (*A Group of Noble Dames*)

Imaginative Woman, An (*Life's Little Ironies*; first published in *Wessex Tales*)

Incident in the Life of Mr. George Crookhill (*Life's Little Ironies*)

Interlopers at the Knap (*Wessex Tales*)

Lady Icenway, The (*A Group of Noble Dames*)

Lady Mottisfont (*A Group of Noble Dames*)

Lady Penelope, The (*A Group of Noble Dames*)

Marchioness of Stonehenge, The (*A Group of Noble Dames*)

Master John Horseleigh, Knight (*A Changed Man*)

Melancholy Hussar of the German Legion, The (*Wessex Tales*; first published in *Life's Little Ironies*)

Mere Interlude, A (*A Changed Man*)

INDEX OF SHORT STORIES

Netty Sargent's Copyhold (*Life's Little Ironies*)

Old Andrey's Experience as a Musician (*Life's Little Ironies*)

On the Western Circuit (*Life's Little Ironies*)

Romantic Adventures of a Milkmaid, The (*A Changed Man*)

Son's Veto, The (*Life's Little Ironies*)

Squire Petrick's Lady (*A Group of Noble Dames*)

Superstitious Man's Story, The (*Life's Little Ironies*)

Three Strangers, The (*Wessex Tales*)

Tony Kytes, the Arch-Deceiver (*Life's Little Ironies*)

To Please his Wife (*Life's Little Ironies*)

Tradition of Eighteen Hundred and Four, A (*Wessex Tales*; first published in *Life's Little Ironies*)

Tragedy of Two Ambitions, A (*Life's Little Ironies*)

Tryst at an Ancient Earthwork, A (*A Changed Man*)

Waiting Supper, The (*A Changed Man*)

What the Shepherd Saw (*A Changed Man*)

Winters and the Palmleys, The (*Life's Little Ironies*)

Withered Arm, The (*Wessex Tales*)

Note: This Index omits four stories (i.e. *Old Mrs. Chundle, The Intruder, Destiny and a Blue Cloak,* and *The Doctor's Legend*) not published in book form during Hardy's lifetime. For details of these see the Select Bibliography above.

WRITERS AND THEIR WORK

Available at 2s. net each; starred titles 1s. 6d. net each

MATTHEW ARNOLD: Kenneth Allott
JANE AUSTEN*: Sylvia Townsend
  Warner
HILAIRE BELLOC: Renée Haynes
ARNOLD BENNETT*: Frank
  Swinnerton
WILLIAM BLAKE*: Kathleen Raine
JAMES BOSWELL: P. A. W. Collins
ELIZABETH BOWEN: Jocelyn Brooke
THE BRONTË SISTERS: P. Bentley
BUNYAN: Henri Talon
SAMUEL BUTLER: G. D. H. Cole
BYRON*: Herbert Read
THOMAS CARLYLE*: D. Gascoyne
JOYCE CARY: Walter Allen
CHAUCER: Nevill Coghill
G. K. CHESTERTON: Christopher Hollis
WINSTON CHURCHILL: John Connell
COLERIDGE: Kathleen Raine
R. G. COLLINGWOOD: E. W. F.
  Tomlin
I. COMPTON-BURNETT*: Pamela
  Hansford Johnson
JOSEPH CONRAD: Oliver Warner
GEORGE CRABBE: R. L. Brett
C. DAY LEWIS: Clifford Dyment
DEFOE*: J. R. Sutherland
CHARLES DICKENS: K. J. Fielding
NORMAN DOUGLAS: Ian Greenlees
JOHN DRYDEN: Bonamy Dobrée
GEORGE ELIOT*: Lettice Cooper
T. S. ELIOT: M. C. Bradbrook
FIELDING: John Butt
FORD MADOX FORD: Kenneth Young
E. M. FORSTER: Rex Warner
CHRISTOPHER FRY: Derek Stanford
EDWARD GIBBON: C. V. Wedgwood
ROBERT GRAVES: M. Seymour-Smith
GRAHAM GREENE: Francis Wyndham
JOHN GALSWORTHY: R. H. Mottram
THOMAS HARDY*: R. A. Scott-James
G. M. HOPKINS: Geoffrey Grigson
A. E. HOUSMAN: Ian Scott-Kilvert
ALDOUS HUXLEY: Jocelyn Brooke
HENRY JAMES: Michael Swan

SAMUEL JOHNSON: S. C. Roberts
JOHN KEATS: Edmund Blunden
RUDYARD KIPLING*: Bonamy
  Dobrée
CHARLES LAMB: Edmund Blunden
D. H. LAWRENCE: Kenneth Young
WYNDHAM LEWIS: E. W. F. Tomlin
KATHERINE MANSFIELD: Ian A.
  Gordon
WALTER DE LA MARE: K. Hopkins
MARLOWE: Philip Henderson
JOHN MASEFIELD*: L. A. G. Strong
SOMERSET MAUGHAM*: J. Brophy
MILTON: E. M. W. Tillyard
WILLIAM MORRIS: Philip Henderson
EDWIN MUIR: J. C. Hall
JOHN HENRY NEWMAN:
  J. M. Cameron
GEORGE ORWELL: Tom Hopkinson
POPE: Ian Jack
HERBERT READ: Francis Berry
RUSKIN: Peter Quennell
BERTRAND RUSSELL*: Alan Dorward
BERNARD SHAW*: A. C. Ward
SHAKESPEARE: C. J. Sisson
SHELLEY: Stephen Spender
SHERIDAN*: W. A. Darlington
EDITH SITWELL: John Lehmann
OSBERT SITWELL*: Roger Fulford
TOBIAS SMOLLETT*: L. Brander
STERNE: D. W. Jefferson
R. L. STEVENSON: G. B. Stern
LYTTON STRACHEY: R. A.
  Scott-James
SWIFT: J. Middleton Murry
SWINBURNE: H. J. C. Grierson
TENNYSON: F. L. Lucas
G. M. TREVELYAN*: J. H. Plumb
EVELYN WAUGH: Christopher Hollis
H. G. WELLS: Montgomery Belgion
OSCAR WILDE: James Laver
CHARLES WILLIAMS: J. Heath-Stubbs
IZAAK WALTON: Margaret Bottrall
VIRGINIA WOOLF: Bernard Blackstone
WORDSWORTH: Helen Darbishire
W. B. YEATS: G. S. Fraser

*The first 55 issues in the Series appeared under the
General Editorship of* T. O. BEACHCROFT

❡ Essays in active preparation include assessments of Spenser, Donne, Burns,
Burke, Dylan Thomas, Edmund Blunden and other classics and contemporaries.

WRITERS AND THEIR WORK

★

A NEW ISSUE in this series on Writers and their
Work is published monthly and may be ordered from
any bookseller or, in case of difficulty, direct from the
Publishers, LONGMANS, GREEN & CO. LTD., 6 &
7 Clifford Street, London W.1.

Annual subscription (12 issues)	22s. 6d. post free
Six months' subscription (6 issues)	12s. post free
Single issues	2s. each

(Back numbers available at 1s. 6d. and 2s. each—for
list of titles see inside cover.)

★

BRITISH BOOK NEWS, to which these essays
form supplements, is published monthly and may be
obtained from The British Council, 65 Davies Street,
London W.1. In addition to an article of general or
bibliographical interest, each issue contains short, infor-
mative and critical reviews, by specialists, of some 200
books. Every subject is covered, including fiction and
children's books, and full details of publisher, price, size,
etc., are given. Annual subscription: U.K. 24s. (or 26s.★);
U.S.A. and Canada $3.50 (or $3.70★); other countries
10s. (or 12s.★).

★ With Annual Index